T0378986

DISASTERS AND THE ENVIRONMENT

EARTHQUAKES
and the Environment

by Jamee-Marie Edwards

CAPSTONE PRESS
a capstone imprint

Published by Capstone Press, an imprint of Capstone
1710 Roe Crest Drive, North Mankato, Minnesota 56003
capstonepub.com

Copyright © 2025 by Capstone. All rights reserved. No part of this publication may be reproduced in whole or in part, or stored in a retrieval system, or transmitted in any form or by any means, electronic, mechanical, photocopying, recording, or otherwise, without written permission of the publisher.

Library of Congress Cataloging-in-Publication Data is available on the Library of Congress website.
ISBN: 9781669070900 (hardcover)
ISBN: 9781669071006 (paperback)
ISBN: 9781669071013 (ebook PDF)

Summary: Huge cracks in highways. Buildings reduced to rubble. An earthquake can leave behind great destruction. These disasters affect the environment too. They can change the coastline, disrupting plant and animal life. They trigger tsunamis and landslides that cause further damage. Learn how people can help affected areas recover from these deadly natural disasters.

Editorial Credits
Editor: Carrie Sheely; Designer: Bobbie Nuytten; Media Researcher: Jo Miller; Production Specialist: Whitney Schaefer

Image Credits
Alamy: Cavan Images, 29, imageBROKER.com GmbH & Co. KG, 20, The Reading Room, 5; Getty Images: AFP, 16, Jorge Villalba, 12, Kyodo News, 24; Science Source: UIG/Philip Wolmuth, 25; Shutterstock: Ammit Jack, Cover (bottom), Breck P. Kent, 7, Daniel Poloha, 18, JAVIER LOCKE, 23, John A. Anderson, 27, Karel Stipek, Cover (top), LouieLea, 17, masami_9625, 15, Molly NZ, 26, NigelSpiers, 11, 21, Peter Hermes Furian, 6, 8, Simone Migliaro, 9, Tamaraklei, 22, traction, 14; Superstock: Design Pics/Peter Langer, 13, Minden Pictures/Flip Nicklin, 19

Design Elements
Shutterstock: klyaksun

Any additional websites and resources referenced in this book are not maintained, authorized, or sponsored by Capstone. All product and company names are trademarks™ or registered® trademarks of their respective holders.

Printed and bound in the USA. PO 5853

TABLE OF CONTENTS

INTRODUCTION
Dust and Dark Skies 4

CHAPTER ONE
Shaking and Shifting............. 6

CHAPTER TWO
Earthquake Environmental
Effects 10

CHAPTER THREE
Effects on Ecosystems.......... 16

CHAPTER FOUR
Bouncing Back................. 24

CHAPTER FIVE
Humans and Earthquakes 28

Glossary 30
Read More 31
Internet Sites 31
Index.................... 32
About the Author 32

Words in **bold** are in the glossary.

Introduction

DUST AND DARK SKIES

In the winter of 1811–1812, a powerful series of earthquakes shook the area near New Madrid, Missouri. The earthquakes received attention for the air **pollution** they caused. **Smog** caused the sky to become darker. It was difficult for people to breathe, and the air had a horrible smell. Scientists think that dust from Earth's surface rose into the air after the earthquakes. It then formed a large cloud.

FACT
The New Madrid earthquakes caused land to shift. This caused the Mississippi River to briefly flow backward.

The New Madrid earthquakes were some of the strongest in U.S. history. But they are also known for how they affected the **environment**. Besides causing air pollution, the earthquakes caused big cracks to open in the ground. Farmland was ruined. The shaking caused trees to fall into the Mississippi River.

During the New Madrid earthquakes, land sank on the eastern side of the Mississippi River. River water rushed in to form Reelfoot Lake in Tennessee.

5

Chapter One

SHAKING AND SHIFTING

An earthquake is a sudden shaking of the ground. Earth's outermost layer is called the crust. Changes in the crust cause most earthquakes. Earth's crust is made up of rock masses called tectonic plates. These plates look like huge puzzle pieces. Tectonic plates are always shifting and moving. They move above and below one another, pull apart, and glide together.

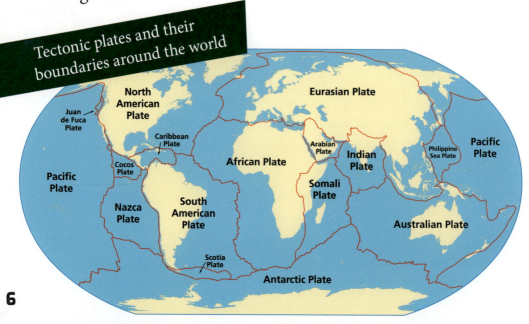

Tectonic plates and their boundaries around the world

FACT

As tectonic plates shift, they can form mountains. The mountains form where two plates collide.

Sometimes two plates get stuck at their edges along plate boundaries. Eventually, this causes a buildup of pressure. When the pressure is released, the plates move quickly. The movement releases energy. Shock waves then move through the rocks and cause the ground to shake. Most earthquakes occur along cracks in Earth's crust called faults.

The San Andreas Fault formed along the boundaries of the Pacific Plate and the North American Plate. Many earthquakes happen along the fault.

Earthquake Hot Spots

About 90 percent of earthquakes occur in a horseshoe-shaped area known as the Pacific Ring of Fire. The Ring of Fire passes through Asia's island regions. It goes along the west coastlines of North and South America. Fifteen countries are in the Ring of Fire, including New Zealand and the United States.

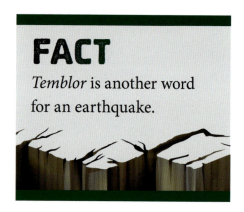

FACT
Temblor is another word for an earthquake.

Many earthquakes are devastating. Buildings can fall down. Roads can be destroyed. Some people may be hurt or killed. But the impact of an earthquake doesn't stop there. Earthquakes have an impact on the environment as well.

In 2016, a powerful earthquake struck central Italy. Nearly 300 people were killed.

Chapter Two

EARTHQUAKE ENVIRONMENTAL EFFECTS

After an earthquake, the environment changes. The impacts an earthquake has on the environment are known as Earthquake Environmental Effects (EEEs). EEEs are divided into two categories called primary and secondary effects.

Primary effects are directly connected to the earthquake source. For example, the ground can be broken up and forced apart during an earthquake. This is known as a surface rupture. Surface ruptures happen along faults.

Secondary effects are caused by the ground shaking, such as landslides and **tsunamis**. Pollution of the air, soil, and water can be among these EEEs.

FACT

On November 14, 2016, an earthquake on New Zealand's South Island caused 112 miles (180 kilometers) of surface ruptures.

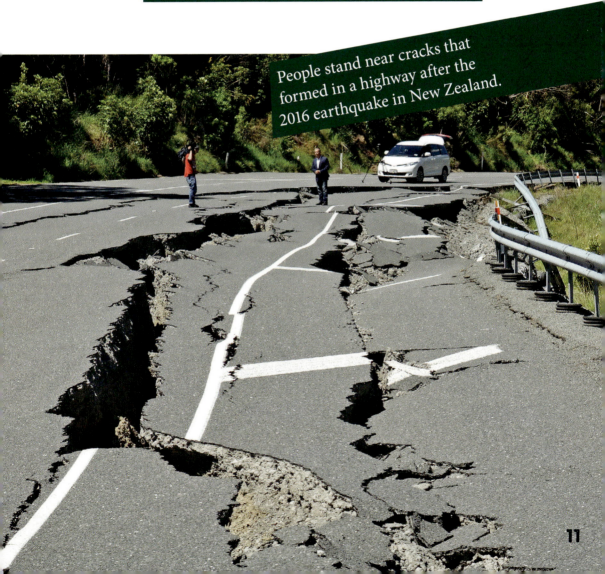

People stand near cracks that formed in a highway after the 2016 earthquake in New Zealand.

Air Pollution

In 1994, an earthquake occurred near Northridge, California. It triggered landslides that caused dust clouds. This led to an outbreak of a lung infection nicknamed "valley fever." The affected residents experienced coughing and fevers. Three people died. A **fungus** normally found in soil caused the disease to spread. The fungi **spores** had gotten into the air after the earthquake.

The 1994 Northridge earthquake caused landslides in the Los Angeles area.

Case Study
2005 Kashmir Earthquake

The Kashmir earthquake shook northern Pakistan on October 8, 2005. It had a negative impact on the country's water supply and sewage system. In many places, the water supply either dried up or was buried by landslides. Some water was polluted with silt and **sediment**. More than 4,000 drinking water supply systems were affected. Drinking polluted water can make people sick.

Soon after, groups made plans to help people. The United Nations Children's Fund (UNICEF) and the Royal Netherlands Embassy (RNE) of Pakistan created one project. People were supplied with packaged water, water filters, and water purification tablets. Organizations also set up water quality testing facilities.

Water Pollution

Earthquakes can also have a negative impact on water quality. For example, ground shaking can loosen sediment from rocks found in wells. This can cause the well water to become cloudy. Ground shaking can also cause sewer lines to break and leak harmful chemicals into the water.

Soil Pollution

Earthquakes also can affect soil. On March 11, 2011, the Tōhoku earthquake caused a massive tsunami in Japan. The soil became polluted with salt that the ocean water left behind. The salt buildup made it difficult for plants to take in water and nutrients. Paddy fields where rice grew made up 85 percent of the damaged farmland. Hills with vegetables such as cabbage and cucumbers made up the remaining 15 percent of the destroyed area.

Japanese farmers plant seedlings in rice paddy fields in spring.

A cabbage field in Miura, Japan

Recovery efforts are actions taken to restore or improve an area affected by a disaster. The time it takes for harmful conditions to improve varies. It can take weeks, months, or years. After the 2011 earthquake in Japan, it took about three years for the affected farmland to become suitable for crop production.

Chapter Three

EFFECTS ON ECOSYSTEMS

A group of animals, plants, and their environment make up an **ecosystem**. Animals can only survive in an ecosystem when their needs are met. When part of an ecosystem is destroyed by an earthquake, the results can be devastating.

Food Shortage

Forests are home to more than 80 percent of land animals, including giant pandas. On May 12, 2008, the Sichuan earthquake in southern China damaged 23 percent of the pandas' **habitat**. Bamboo is the main part of a panda's diet. Special food had to be prepared for the pandas in the Wolong Nature Reserve because of a bamboo shortage.

Workers feed giant pandas at the Wolong Nature Reserve after the 2008 earthquake.

FACT

Giant pandas are **endangered**. Only about 1,800 giant pandas are left in the wild.

Coastal Ecosystem Wonder

Earthquakes have the power to change the shape and level of the seafloor. On November 14, 2016, the Kaikōura earthquake rattled the northeastern coast of New Zealand's South Island. The earthquake raised some underwater areas of the seafloor by 18 feet (5.5 meters) and changed the coastline.

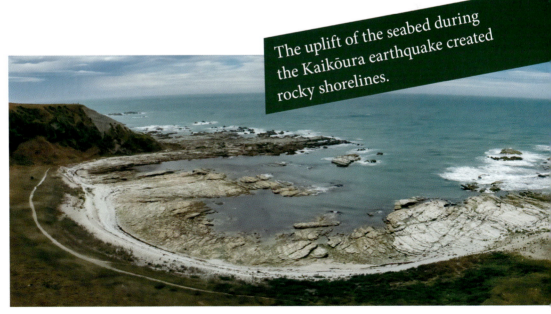

The uplift of the seabed during the Kaikōura earthquake created rocky shorelines.

The changed coastline resulted in a loss of kelp forests. Large brown **algae** make up kelp forests. Kelp forests are the foundation of a healthy ecosystem. They provide homes and food for sea creatures, including sea snails called paua. Many paua were pushed out of the water when the land shifted. After the earthquake, many fisheries closed to protect paua. Some fisheries remained closed until 2021.

Kelp forests grow along coastlines around the world.

Conservationists were concerned about the impact the changed coastline would have on Hector's dolphins. Hector's dolphins rely on shorelines for finding food. These dolphins live mainly around New Zealand's coast. A survey was conducted on Hector's dolphins after the earthquake. Thankfully, the study showed no major changes in the number of dolphins for two years after the earthquake.

Hector's dolphins are one of the smallest dolphins. Their rounded dorsal fin sets them apart from many other dolphins.

Destroyed Seabird Nests

The Kaikōura earthquake caused about 100,000 landslides. The Kaikōura mountains were one of the areas affected by the landslides. This range is home to the world's two remaining natural colonies of endangered Hutton's shearwater seabirds. People inspected each of these seabirds' nests six months after the earthquake. They found that about half of the nests had been destroyed. They estimated that about half of the nesting chicks had died.

Hutton's shearwater seabirds swim near South Island, New Zealand.

The Kaikōura mountains stretch along 60 miles (97 km) of South Island's northeastern coast.

A New Home

Researchers have discovered earthquakes can sometimes help animals. The change in the seafloor caused by the Kaikōura earthquake created new places for fur seals to live. The seals started to live in new areas in Ohau Point, New Zealand.

Sperm Whales

Sperm whales are the largest of the toothed whales and dolphins. They can be seen close to the shoreline in Kaikōura, New Zealand, year-round. They eat deep-sea squid and fish.

In 1990, Steve Dawson and Liz Slooten started a research program on sperm whales in Kaikōura. When the Kaikōura earthquake struck, researchers were able to conduct the first specialized study on the impact of earthquakes on marine animals. Sperm whales were impacted by the earthquake because they had to dive deeper and longer to locate food. A year after the earthquake, researchers discovered the whales had returned to their normal patterns.

Sperm whales usually surface about once every hour to breathe.

Erosion Problems

On April 16, 2016, an earthquake struck Ecuador's coast. The local forest animals suffered after the earthquake caused erosion. Erosion happens when tiny pieces of Earth's surface move from one place to another. Many ground animal habitats were damaged or lost because of the land changes.

Thick forests along Ecuador's coastline are home to a variety of wildlife.

Chapter Four

BOUNCING BACK

Ecosystem restoration is a process that helps an ecosystem work as it did before a disaster. This can mean changing it back to the way it was or helping it adapt to new conditions. Ecosystem restoration also helps protect ecosystems from harm.

People work to reforest trees in Japan after the 2011 earthquake.

Why do ecosystems need to be restored? Healthy ecosystems bring many advantages. They help keep our water and air clean. They are home to various plant and animal life, including plants used for medications. Ecosystem restoration can be done in different ways.

Reforestation can occur where there were forests. It involves planting trees. People try to plant a variety of native species as well as rare and endangered species.

Case Study
2010 Haiti Earthquake

On January 12, 2010, an earthquake in Port-au-Prince, Haiti, triggered tens of thousands of landslides. Many trees were destroyed. The Haitian American Tree Trust was created to help in the recovery process. On May 1, 2013, people in Haiti took part in a large tree-planting event. About 1.2 million trees were planted that day.

Tree saplings planted as part of a reforestation project in Haiti

Rewilding can be used to restore various ecosystems, such as wetlands and forests. It can include reintroducing creatures such as beavers or wolves to an area. The goal is for people to help get nature to a point where it can take care of itself.

Efforts focus on restoring the area's native species. Replanting can assist with recovery. For example, after the 2016 earthquake in New Zealand, 95 percent of the country's Ōhau Point daisy population was destroyed. A group called the North Canterbury Transport Infrastructure Recovery assisted in the collection of daisy seeds for replanting.

The Ōhau Point daisy grows only on rock faces north of Kaikōura.

Case Study
2009 Honduras Earthquake

In 2009, an earthquake off the coast of Honduras damaged the coral reefs of the Belize Barrier Reef lagoon. In 2010, Dr. Richard Aronson of the Florida Institute of Technology and several of his coworkers visited 21 reef sites. They discovered almost 50 percent of the reef slopes had fallen into deeper water. Only sediment and coral skeletons remained.

In 2009, the Belize Barrier Reef Reserve System was added to the United Nations Education Scientific and Cultural Organization's (UNESCO) List of World Heritage in Danger. However, in 2018 the reef was taken off the list as a result of conservation efforts. A group called Fragments of Hope helped with coral reef restoration. The group uses corals raised in artificial nurseries to reseed damaged areas. More than 100,000 corals have been reseeded.

Healthy coral supports a variety of sea life.

Chapter Five

HUMANS AND EARTHQUAKES

Earthquakes can cause loss of life and property damage. The earthquake that struck Haiti in 2010 claimed 250,000 lives and caused major damage to homes. Recovery from so much damage can take many years. Habitat for Humanity created a five-year plan to help people rebuild their homes. The organization assisted about 40,000 families with a place to live.

Emotional Impact

Handling stress and anxiety is often hard for disaster survivors. After an earthquake, both adults and children experience emotional pain, loss, and fear. Some people develop a condition called Post Traumatic Stress Disorder (PTSD). According to a study, one out of every four people experienced PTSD following the 2010 earthquake in Haiti.

The Recovery Process

After an earthquake, the recovery process starts. People begin to rebuild structures. They work to help affected ecosystems. Yet it can take many years for an ecosystem to fully recover. Ocean ecosystems can often recover in about 10 years. Forest ecosystems often need about 42 years to recover. Efforts may be affected by environmental changes, such as global warming. It may not be possible for an ecosystem to return to its original condition.

Scientists continue to study earthquake recovery processes. After every disaster, they put what they've learned into practice to get the best outcomes.

Earthquake researchers install a seismometer to measure ground movement in California.

Glossary

algae (AL-jee)—small plants without roots or stems that grow in water

conservationist (kahn-sur-VAY-shuh-nist)—a person who works to protect natural resources

ecosystem (EE-koh-sis-tuhm)—a group of animals and plants that work together with their surroundings

endangered (in-DAYN-juhrd)—at risk of dying out

environment (in-VY-ruhn-muhnt)—the natural world of the land, water, and air

fungus (FUHN-guhs)— a single-celled organism that lives by breaking down and absorbing the natural material it lives in

habitat (HAB-uh-tat)—the natural place and conditions in which a plant or animal lives

pollution (puh-LOO-shuhn)—materials that hurt Earth's water, air, and land

sediment (SED-uh-muhnt)—rocks, sand, or dirt that has been carried to a place by water, wind, or a glacier

smog (SMOG)—a mixture of fog and smoke

spore (SPOR)—a cell of a living thing that develops into a new living thing

tsunami (tsoo-NAH-mee)—a gigantic ocean wave created by an undersea earthquake, landslide, or volcanic eruption

Read More

Golkar, Golriz. *Earthquakes.* North Mankato, MN: Capstone, 2022.

Romero, Libby. *All About Earthquakes: Discovering How Earth Moves and Shakes.* New York: Children's Press, 2022.

Van Rose, Susanna. *Volcano & Earthquake.* New York: DK Publishing, 2022.

Internet Sites

NASA Space Place: What Is an Earthquake?
spaceplace.nasa.gov/earthquakes/en/#:~:text=An%20
earthquake%20is%20an%20intense,movements%20in%20
Earth%27s%20outermost%20layer

National Geographic Kids: Earthquakes
kids.nationalgeographic.com/science/article/earthquake

USGS: Cool Earthquake Facts
usgs.gov/programs/earthquake-hazards/cool-earthquake-facts

Index

air pollution, 4, 5, 10, 12

emotional impacts, 28

faults, 7, 10

giant pandas, 16, 17

Haiti, 25, 28
Hector's dolphins, 19
Honduras, 27
Hutton's shearwater seabirds, 20

Kashmir earthquake, 13
kelp forests, 18

landslides, 10, 12, 13, 20, 25
lung infections, 12

mountains, 7, 20, 21

New Madrid earthquakes, 4, 5

New Zealand, 8, 11, 17, 19, 20, 21, 22, 26

reforestation, 25
rewilding, 26
Ring of Fire, 8

soil pollution, 10, 14
sperm whales, 22

tectonic plates, 6, 7
tsunamis, 10, 14

water pollution, 10, 13

About the Author

Photo credit Clifford Mason MASEfx

Jamee-Marie Edwards is an author, STEAM educator, literacy advocate, and nurse from New York City. She is the founder of The Me I Need to Be program and uses the arts and sciences to empower children. Learn more about Jamee-Marie at her website maeinspireu.com.